Plato's Republic

Text by
Tonnvane Wiswell
M.A., Arizona State University

Dr. M. Fogiel
Chief Editor

Illustrations by
Karen Pica

Research & Education Association

MAXnotes® for
PLATO'S REPUBLIC

Printed in the United States of America

Library of Congress Catalog Card Number 98-66192

International Standard Book Number 0-87891-987-2

MAXnotes® is a registered trademark of
Research & Education Association, Piscataway, New Jersey 08854

What MAXnotes® Will Do for You

This book is intended to help you absorb the essential contents and features of *Plato's Republic* and to help you gain a thorough understanding of the work. This **MAXnotes** study guide has been designed to enable you to do this more quickly and effectively than any other study guide.

For best results, this **MAXnotes** book should be used as a companion to—not as a substitute for—the actual work. The interaction between the two will greatly benefit you.

To help you in your studies, this book presents the most up-to-date interpretations of every section of the actual work, followed by questions and fully explained answers that will enable you to analyze the material critically. The questions also will help you to test your understanding of the work and will prepare you for discussions and exams.

Meaningful illustrations are included to further enhance your understanding and enjoyment of the literary work.

The **MAXnotes** study guides also include summaries, character lists, explanations of plot, and section-by-section analyses. A biography of the author and discussion of the work's historical context will help you put this literary piece into the proper perspective of what is taking place.

The use of this study guide will save you the hours of preparation time that would ordinarily be required to arrive at a complete grasp of this work of literature. You will be well prepared for classroom discussions, homework, and exams. The guidelines that are included for writing papers and reports on various topics will prepare you for any added work which may be assigned.

The **MAXnotes** will take your grades "to the max."

Dr. Max Fogiel
Program Director

MAXnotes® are simply the best –
but don't just take our word for it...

"... I have told every bookstore in the area to carry your MAXnotes. They are the only notes I recommend to my students. There is no comparison between MAXnotes and all other notes ..."
— *High School Teacher & Reading Specialist,*
Arlington High School, Arlington, MA

"... I discovered the MAXnotes when a friend loaned me her copy of the MAXnotes for Romeo and Juliet. The book really helped me understand the story. Please send me a list of stores in my area that carry the MAXnotes. I would like to use more of them ..."
— *Student, San Marino, CA*

"... The two MAXnotes titles that I have used have been very, very, helpful in helping me understand the subject matter reviewed. Thank you for creating the MAXnotes series ..."
— *Student, Morrisville, PA*

Contents

Each of the following Books includes List of Characters, Summary, Analysis, Study Questions and Answers, and Suggested Essay Topics.

Introduction

The Life and Work of Plato

As a citizen of Athens, Plato's life was a product of a society dominated by war outside of the state and the direct practice of democracy within it. Above and beyond these influences, however, one must turn to Plato's mentor Socrates (469–399 B.C.) to understand Plato's thought.

Socrates was the self-appointed gadfly of Athens. Avoiding the Assembly in favor of more private audiences, he questioned and occasionally ridiculed the assumptions upon which Athenians built their beliefs. While this won Socrates many young followers, it also earned him numerous enemies. This led to his being brought to trial on charges of impiety and corrupting the youth of Athens in 399 B.C.. His defense, recorded in Plato's *Apology*, failed to sway the jury in his favor, and he was condemned to death. While he could have escaped, Socrates chose death.

Socrates' death was the major formative event in Plato's youth, turning him away from politics and toward philosophy. His early writings, primarily records of the words of Socrates (Tredennick, 1969), displayed Socrates' famed teaching method of conducting informal question-and-answer sessions with small groups of men. As Plato progressed, he continued to use Socrates as the main character in his dialogues, although the thoughts he expressed became Plato's own.

After spending more than a decade away from Athens after Socrates' death, Plato eventually returned to found the Academy. There he attempted to turn aspiring politicians into "philosophic

statesmen" (Cornford, in Lee, 1974). He also attempted to turn kings toward philosophy, both through correspondence and personal visits to their courts (Lee, 1974). Plato died in Athens in 347 B.C., leaving behind the unfinished manuscript to *The Laws.*

Historical Background

It is difficult to imagine what a great gap divides the modern world and the society of ancient Greece. Though united by language and a feeling of superiority over all those who did not speak Greek—the "barbarians"—the ancient Greeks were not united amongst themselves. Each valley could and often did support its own independent political community; even an island often had more than one self-ruled city-state (Greek *polis*).With so much fragmentation, it is unsurprising that the Greek communities fought each other. This, and the greedy designs of neighboring kingdoms, made war a part of the culture of ancient Greece.

Yet within the polis, citizens met together and mutually decided how their community would deal with the problems it faced. The small size was beneficial insofar as it allowed the kind of direct contact necessary for its inhabitants to rule themselves. The existence of citizen rule among the Greeks contrasted strongly with the absolute monarchies other Mediterranean peoples endured, further solidifying the sense of Greek identity (Finley, 1964).

Some unity finally emerged among the eastern city-states in response to Persia's attempt to invade mainland Greece after successfully bringing those in Asia Minor under its control. Athens was primarily responsible for defeating the Persians in 490 B.C., and the Athenians followed their victory in 480 at the head of a small coalition of city-states. Anticipating a third attack, Athens formed a confederation out of the frightened Greek states, which made contributions to Athens for mutual defense.

After the Persian fleet was eliminated, the members of the "Delian League" wished to resume their autonomy, but Athens forcibly chose to maintain and even expand the alliance, changing it from a confederation into an empire. Enriched by the continuing tribute, Athens came to be seen as a threat by Sparta, leader of the Peloponnesian League. This eventually led to the quarter-century series of battles known as the Peloponnesian War, which ended in 404 B.C. with Athens' defeat and the dissolution of its empire. Although Athens was able to regain control over itself, it was weakened, and the anarchy that reigned in areas it had formerly controlled set the stage for Athens' own final fall to the Macedonians in 322 B.C. (Finley, 1964).

While the members of the Delian League benefitted from the general peace imposed by Athens, it was Athens that benefitted most. This time became known as its Golden Age. Credit for much of Athens' accomplishments during this period is often given to its leader, Pericles, who took the impressive sums stockpiled at the Acropolis, satisfied himself that the Athenian fleet was strong, and applied the money to improving his city (Kitto, 1957). Under his leadership rose the Parthenon, a public-works project on the grandest of scales. In addition to increasing spending on public festivals, Pericles also instituted a system of pay for attendance at the Assembly, which expanded democratic participation beyond the leisured classes to the common man.

Democratic practice in Athens is criticized today for its lack of inclusiveness. Out of a population of approximately 250,000, the polis of Athens harbored approximately 70,000 slaves, who provided much of the opportunity for leisure that direct democracy required to exist. In addition to the exclusion of the numerous aliens, women were completely excluded from political life. This left about 40,000 to 50,000 adult male citizens as potential participants in Athens' rule.

Rather than criticize Athens for those it excluded, it is more instructive to look at how those who were eligible participated in its rule. Any (male) citizen could attend the Assembly and vote on the matters being debated there; any man who felt confident enough could speak in debate; and, finally, all but a few offices in the government were filled, not by elections, but by lot. Given the energy this form of government required, it is unsurprising that the culture of Athens was utterly dominated by the existence of democracy. While Athens' government was criticized for its imperfections at the time—perhaps most eloquently by Plato—the Athenian experiment embodies ideals of participation to which moderns can but aspire.

Ancient Greece

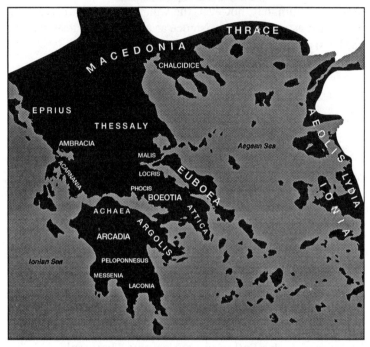

Reactions to The Republic

The most famous critique of *The Republic* from one of Plato's contemporaries came from Aristotle, who, in his *Politics*, dismissed *The Republic* out of hand for making proposals that were contrary to human nature. Aristotle was especially critical of Plato's assertion that women, children, and property would best be held in common by the Guardians (*Politics*, Book II).

Modern critics still debate the meaning of *The Republic*, some dismissing the elements Aristotle criticized as obvious jokes, others seeing them as providing fundamental insights into the malleability of human "nature." Plato has also alternately been criticized as utopian and authoritarian: Some find his proposals impossible, while others find them likely to create a fascist state.

The Republic's role as a classic of Western literature is unquestioned. Many of the metaphors and parables Plato uses within it are referred to frequently, most especially the Allegory of the Cave (Book 7). Ultimately, however, the value of *The Republic* can be found just as much in its existence as a source of questions as it has been a source of answers.

Master List of Characters

Socrates—*narrator of the book.*

Glaucon—*son of Ariston (and brother of Plato, who does not appear). Presents the view that justice is something the weak attempt to force on the strong.*

Adeimantus—*brother of Glaucon. Describes justice as accomplished for its practical benefits. He and Glaucon are the only ones who respond to Socrates' questions after Book I.*

Polemarchus—*host to the gathering at which Socrates speaks. He describes justice as giving others what they deserve.*

Cephalus—*elderly gentleman, Polemarchus' father. He defines justice as honesty and returning what one takes from others.*

Thrasymachus—*teacher of rhetoric ("sophist"). He argues the position that might makes right.*

Cleitophon, Lysias, Euthydemus, Niceratus, Charmanides—*other guests at Polemarchus'.*

Summary of the Work

Socrates, visiting Polemarchus' house, enters into a conversation on the nature of justice. Several different definitions are presented by the various guests. After finding each of these lacking, Socrates attempts to define justice himself. This requires that he first describe justice on the scale of the state (or "the republic"). Here, Socrates finds justice to be each person performing the task at which he[1] excels.

Since the modern "fevered" state necessitates soldiers, Socrates asserts that a method must be found to ensure that they do their

---

[1] Because of the exclusion of women from Greek political life, "he or she" is not used unless applicable.

job well. He then lays out a system of education that will make them the best possible soldiers. Out of this well-disciplined group, the rulers of society—the Guardians—will be chosen. The goal of society will be the happiness of the community, a goal that will be achieved because of the beliefs held by the various classes.

After discussing the role of philosophy and the philosopher in society, Socrates concludes that the philosopher would be the ideal ruler. Socrates uses the parable of the ship of state, the simile of the divided line, and the allegory of the cave to express the philosopher's ability to see the truth and use this knowledge to guide the state. Socrates then discusses the various inferior forms government can take, concluding that a despotic government is worst, with democracy only slightly better.

Returning to the question of justice, Socrates asserts that the just life is happier and justice leads to a profitable life. Following the path of justice makes society better, and the gods reward a just man. Asserting the existence of a soul, Socrates tells his final parable, the Myth of Ur. This enables him to show that the benefits of justice continue in the afterlife, where the unjust are punished and repeat the mistakes they made on earth. In conclusion, Socrates finds that virtue and the good life are indeed profitable, in this world and the next.

Estimated Reading Time

Although *The Republic*'s conversational style makes it surprisingly easy to read, some sections are difficult to digest. In addition, taking time to reflect on the work as one reads it aids comprehension.

For this reason, a good understanding of the book necessitates it be read in at least two sittings. For a reader who is generally unfamiliar with the ideas presented in *The Republic*, four sittings would not be unreasonable.

Suggested breaks	Approximate reading time
Books I–III	90 minutes
Books IV–VI	2 hours
Books VII–VIII	90 minutes
Books IX–X	90 minutes

These breaks are easily digestible, with the important elements of the book distributed evenly among them.

NOTE: Quotes within this work are from the second (1991) edition of Allan Bloom's 1968 translation. While the ten "books" follow the original limitations of papyrus transcription, the line numbers refer to the customary breaks of Stephanus's 1578 edition, included in almost every version of *The Republic*. The work starts at line 327; breaks between books are occasionally discontinuous.

Book One

1. Introduction: Cephalus and the Conventional View of Justice (327–331d)

Summary

While walking back to town with Glaucon, Socrates is invited to spend the evening at Polemarchus' house. Upon arrival, Socrates and Polemarchus' father, Cephalus, discuss the changes that occur with age. Cephalus says he is happy to be free of the passions of youth, adding that age is an easy burden to bear for those who are "sensible and good-tempered" (329d). With prodding from Socrates, Cephalus goes on to say that he is happy that he is well-off, insofar as it has made it easier for him to avoid wrongdoing. This knowledge gives him peace, because he is unafraid of what his judgment will be in the world of the dead.

Socrates then asks Cephalus if it is sufficient to say that one has lived justly merely if one has been truthful and returned what one has borrowed. When Cephalus agrees, Socrates presents the question of returning a weapon to a man gone mad. Since obeying Cephalus' definition of justice would produce a bad result, Socrates finds Cephalus' definition insufficient.

Polemarchus interrupts, saying his father's definition is correct. Cephalus takes this opportunity to depart, leaving his son to continue the argument.

Analysis

In this section, justice, the main topic of *The Republic*, is introduced casually by Cephalus. Socrates will later find justice valuable in the individual insofar as it enables him to control his passions, as Cephalus has done, and praise justice for its value in the afterlife, as Cephalus now does. But while Cephalus' life epitomizes that of a just man in normal society, Socrates finds that he has not really reflected on justice.

Notice the references to sayings of the poets. In a society in which books were an oddity, poetry was a major part of a young man's education. Most revered of the poets was Homer, author of *The Iliad* and *The Odyssey*, who was referred to simply as "the poet." His *Iliad* served the Greeks as a combination of the Bible and the works of Shakespeare.

Socrates' "kidnapping" to Polemarchus' house foreshadows the debate that will later take place between Socrates and Thrasymachus. Superior force convinces Socrates to accompany Polemarchus' party, but Socrates offers debate as a method of ensuring his escape.

2. The Conventional View of Justice Continued: Polemarchus (331e–336a)

Summary

Elaborating on his father's position, Polemarchus asserts that "it is just to give to each what is owed," shortly amending himself to say it is just to do good to one's friends and evil to one's enemies (331e). Socrates then compares justice to a variety of skills, asking Polemarchus if his definition holds true in different situations, such as war, peace, and misinformation. By eliminating what it is not, Socrates makes Polemarchus concede that his definition is not only incorrect, but that following it would foster injustice.

Analysis

In this passage, Socrates briefly introduces the difference between seeming and being, a distinction that will re-emerge when he presents the argument in favor of philosophers as good rulers.

Most of this part of the dialogue consists of similes comparing the proper practice of various skills to the proper practice of justice. The failings of Polemarchus' definition of justice are brought out in this classic example of the Socratic method, which results in convincing Polemarchus himself that he is wrong.

3. Thrasymachus: Justice as the Interest of the Stronger (336b–342e)

Summary

Thrasymachus impatiently interrupts Socrates and Polemarchus, demanding that Socrates stop asking questions and explain his own views on justice. Thrasymachus then challenges Socrates to hear him out. After being assured his payment for teaching, Thrasymachus states that "the just is nothing other than the advantage of the stronger" (338c). He uses the example of two governments that give different laws because they are ruled in different ways, but that are similar in that both states' laws are to the advantage of those who are in power.

Socrates defeats Thrasymachus' argument by pointing out that imperfect knowledge may cause rulers to make laws that are not to their advantage, so that having the subjects justly follow laws may result in an unjust consequence. Switching to an argument centering on the practice of various skills, Socrates shows that insofar as justice is a skill, it is practiced for the benefit of those who are ruled rather than those who rule.

Angered by what he considers an unfair argument, Thrasymachus insults Socrates. He then amends his argument, splitting (or abandoning) his definition of justice in order to assert that the "just" (good) man is exploited by the unjust man. Indeed, the man who is able to act perfectly unjustly, thus becoming a tyrant, is referred to as "happy and fortunate," not only by his countrymen but also by all others (344c). Thrasymachus concludes that injustice is "mightier, freer, and more masterful than justice." (344c)

Socrates undermines Thrasymachus' argument first by arguing that the unjust man is not only bad but ignorant. He then says that the unjust man would be incapable of concerted action.

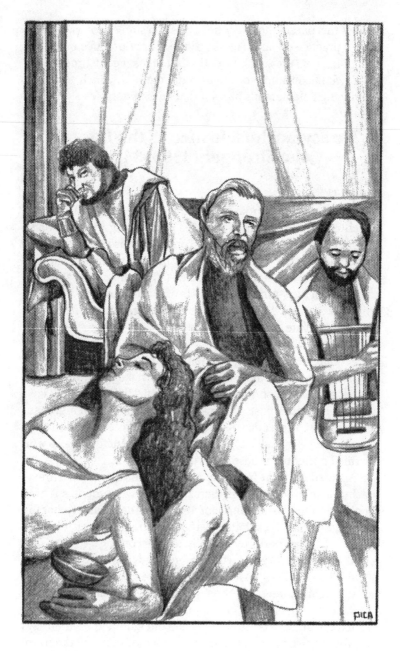

Finally, by defining justice as the virtue of the soul—the element needed for it to accomplish its work well—Socrates shows that the unjust man will never be able to live well and will therefore always be unhappy.

Analysis

The argument in this passage is difficult to follow, in part because of its use of Greek words that translate ambiguously into English, but also because parts of it are, according to one analysis, "embarrassingly bad" (Cross and Woozley, 1964: cited in Lee, 1974:90).

The primary translation problem is found in the word "justice." At times it translates best as "right," as in proper; at other times as "good," as in moral; still again as "natural," as in normal; and finally in the judgment-related sense as it is used most frequently as in English. These ambiguities are what enables Thrasymachus to say that it is just for the strong to dominate the weak, in this sense referring to what is natural. Yet, when he talks about the just being unhappy, he is referring to the man who is morally just.

This passage heavily utilizes similes based in ancient Greek culture. Especially noticeable are the references to sailing. Their pervasiveness is most appropriate in a work of this period, given the Athenian navy's role in Athens' rise to power, as well as the ubiquitous nature of sailing in Mediterranean culture.

Study Questions

1. What are the two views of justice asserted in Book One?

2. For whose benefit does a just ruler rule, according to Socrates?

3. How does Thrasymachus say people view the life of a tyrant?

4. Why has living a just life given Cephalus peace of mind in his old age?

5. What example does Socrates use to show that giving back what one has taken can be an unjust act?

6. Why does being bad to one's enemies result in injustice, according to Socrates?

7. What virtue is necessary for the soul to perform its work well?

8. What reward does the just man seek for ruling?

9. How will a just ruler deal with other states, according to Thrasymachus?

10. List the two examples Socrates gives of making mistakes through mistaking what seems to be for what is.

Answers

1. The two views of justice asserted in Book One are the conventional view of justice, which only requires giving others what they are due, and Thrasymachus' view of justice, which is best summarized in the phrase "might makes right."

2. Socrates says that a just ruler rules for the benefit of his subjects.

3. Thrasymachus says that people consider a tyrant to be happy and blessed.

4. Cephalus has peace of mind because he has no fear of how he will be judged in the world of the dead.

5. Socrates gives the example of a madman asking to have his weapon back as a case where a man who returned what he had borrowed would be acting unjustly.

6. Since being bad to someone could only make them worse, treating even an enemy badly could only result in injustice.

7. According to Socrates, the soul needs justice in order to do its work.

8. The just man only rules for fear of being ruled by someone worse than himself.

9. A just ruler will seek to dominate other states.

10. The first example Socrates gives is with Polemarchus (354). When Polemarchus asserts that it is just to harm one's enemies, Socrates points out that one might, by this course of

action, harm someone who *seems* to be an enemy but is actually a friend. Similarly, when arguing with Thrasymachus over in whose interest laws are passed, Socrates shows that it is possible for a ruler to pass laws that *seem* to be in his interest, thus producing an unjust result, according to Thrasymachus' definition.

Suggested Essay Topics

1. Using "natural" as the definition of just, construct an argument in favor of the rule of the tyrant, drawing upon Thrasymachus' arguments.

2. Which of the definitions of justice presented in this section do you find most compelling? Explain them, comparing their relative advantages and disadvantages.

Book Two

1. Justice as a Convenience (357–367e)

Summary

Glaucon, playing devil's advocate, argues that justice is a good that is unenthusiastically practiced for the benefits it brings. Justice and law are established by men acting in common in order to avoid being on the receiving end of injustice. Glaucon gives the story of Gyges' ring of invisibility to show that every man would prefer to act unjustly if removed from fear of punishment, adding that anyone who didn't would be considered an idiot.

Glaucon then contrasts the life of a perfectly unjust man with a reputation for being just to the life of a perfectly just man with a reputation for injustice. Glaucon says it is clear that the just man will be miserable and the unjust blessed, proving that it is better to *seem* rather than to *be* just; and, thanks to the unjust man's ability to propitiate the gods, he will be favored by them as well.

Adeimantus joins in, arguing that justice is valued for the benefits that come from it: first, from the good reputation it gives; and second, for the blessings it leads the gods to bestow in this life and the next. He concludes by asking Socrates, who has spent his life studying this matter, to compare justice to injustice, showing that justice is superior, not by virtue of its material benefits, but by virtue of its positive effect on a man's soul.

Analysis

According to Desmond Lee, Plato here returns to Thrasymachus' arguments because "the view which he represents needs a clearer statement and a fairer treatment" (Lee, 1974:102). This gives Socrates an opportunity to defeat Thrasymachus' views through more than rationalization.

While expanding Thrasymachus' basic argument, Glaucon adds to it what would now be called a "social contract" explanation for the origin of justice. Its story of a people choosing obedience to the law as preferable to anarchy and injustice is not unique (see Hobbes' *The Leviathan*), but the idea of the people themselves making these laws is—especially at this time—typically Greek.

This section also provides an arena for Plato to discuss the question of reputation. Throughout his works, Plato criticizes the great importance Athenians placed on good reputation and appearance. Plato preferred that people focus on who they are inside rather than wasting time worrying about what other people thought of them.

2. Primitive Social Organization: The City of Pigs (368–372d)

Summary

Socrates decides to first examine justice on the scale of the community. Socrates claims that society is formed because individuals are not self-sufficient. Within the social context, it is best that each member practice the single skill at which he excels. The town is allowed simple craftsmen, farmers, laborers, and merchants, and Socrates lays out for them a simple life that they will enjoy in "peace and health." (372d)

Analysis

The life that Socrates sketches in these passages is seen critically by Glaucon, who shortly refers to it as a city of pigs (or sows). For the highly civilized Athenians (and for moderns), a life devoid

of such small luxuries as plates, furniture, and meat would seem
more like an animal's life than a Greek's.

Even so, this city of simple tastes is Socrates' vision of a healthy
society—not Athens. The maligned city of pigs stands favorably
contrasted to the luxury-ridden "fevered" state described next.

3. Civilized Society: Introduction of Guardians (372e–374e)

Summary

To meet Glaucon's desire for a more civilized society, Socrates
introduces luxury to his state. To support the influx of craftsmen
and the expanded desires of the townsfolk, the state must be en-
larged. Socrates says this can be done only by taking land from
someone else, which will lead to war. Following the principle of
specialization, Socrates insists that a separate class of soldiers will
also become necessary. Socrates therefore proposes to determine
what type of character is required of those chosen to guard the
city—the Guardians.

Analysis

In looking at the need for a class of soldiers, Socrates refers to
his initial arguments in favor of specialization. His recommendations run counter to the Athenian practice of considering every
citizen a potential soldier. The Romans also valued the citizen-sol-
dier, whose apotheosis was Cincinnatus, who returned from glory
on the battlefield to till his farm.

4. Qualities of the Guardians (375–376c)

Summary

Socrates says that a member of the city's Guardians should
have the same qualities as a good watchdog—strength, courage,
and loyalty. In the Guardian's need to be both gentle with his fellows and dangerous to enemies, Socrates finds that he, like the dog,
needs a philosophic nature.

Analysis

This passage is built around an extended simile between a good soldier and a good watchdog. The requirement that a soldier be a philosopher, a crucial assumption for many of the following passages, is introduced as a pun. As discussed by Desmond Lee (1974), it centers around the words *philosophos* (love of learning) and *philomathos* (love of knowledge). Since the dog loves those he knows, he has a love of knowledge and, it follows, a philosophic nature as well. Thus, like the dog, the Guardian must be "by nature a philosopher and a lover of learning" to ensure that he is "gentle to his own." (376c)

5. Educating the Guardians: Poetry (376d–383)

Summary

Socrates examines the proper education of the Guardian. Setting aside physical training, he focuses on the formation of the mind. Since the stories children are told leave strong impressions. they must be regulated. Socrates says that any tale that misrepresents the nature of gods or heroes must be forbidden, citing certain tales from the *Iliad* and other sources as offensive.

Children must learn that the gods are the cause of only good things, not evil; those who are punished by the gods need and benefit from it.

Stories depicting the gods changing shape or disguising themselves will also be banned, not only because it is logically impossible for a god to want to be anything less than his perfect form, but because such stories make children cowardly. Those poets who represent a god in a forbidden manner will not be allowed to present their work, which will also be kept away from children so as not to corrupt them.

Analysis

Socrates' focus on poetry seems quite extreme by modern standards. Whether or not Plato correctly judged its effect on the character, the weight he gives it is entirely appropriate given its importance in Greek culture. For this reason, it seems odd that Socrates' proposals meet with so little resistance from his interlocutors. An excellent argument against these recommendations is made by Aristotle in his *Poetics*, in which he argues that, rather than being disruptive to the well-run state, drama and poetry are beneficent and purgative.

Socrates' argument about truth and falsehood is difficult to understand because of the ambiguous meaning of the Greek word *pseudos*, which translates as "lie" as well as "fiction." Keep this in mind when analyzing the passage.

Study Questions

1. What kind of good does Socrates say justice is?

2. Does Glaucon believe men are at heart good or evil? How does he illustrate his point?

3. Why does Socrates look at the community first?

4. Why does Socrates say people decide to live together, rather than atomistically?

5. Why does Socrates believe people should focus their energies on one activity exclusively?

6. Why must the fevered city have soldiers?

7. Why does Glaucon consider Socrates' healthy city a city of pigs?

8. Why will Socrates not allow tales of battle among the gods?

9. What practical service does a philosophic nature provide in a Guardian?

10. Why does Glaucon say people agree to live under law?

Answers

1. Socrates says justice is a good that is valued for its own sake, not for what it can provide.

2. Glaucon believes men are inherently evil. The story of Gyges' ring illustrates his belief.

3. Socrates looks at the comunity first in order to see justice more clearly by looking at it on the large scale.

4. Socrates says people live together because they are not self-sufficient.

5. Socrates says people should focus their energies on one activity exclusively because usually people have an aptitude for only one activity, they will produce better goods by specializing, and to not engage in that activity could result in missing the right moment for action.

6. Because the fevered city must expand its territory, it must go to war with its neighbors, and therefore it needs soldiers.

7. Glaucon considers the first city a city of pigs because they have no trappings of civilization, such as furniture.

8. According to Socrates, the gods are by nature good. Furthermore, the citizens must learn that quarreling is sinful.

9. A philosophic nature makes a Guardian gentle to those whom he knows.

10. Glaucon says that people agree to live under law because it keeps them from being the victim of injustice at another's hand.

Suggested Essay Topics

1. What argument supports Socrates' desire for a separate class of soldiers? Why might this be a bad idea? What other reasons might support it?

2. What elements of a child's life are most influential on its character? Is Socrates right about the need to control the type of stories a child hears?

Book Three

1. Educating the Guardians: Failings of Poetry (386–392c)

Summary

Socrates adds that, because bravery in war is necessary, children must not be taught to be afraid of death. Stories that portray "Hades' domain" as "full of terror" will be banned, as well as laments by heroes (386b). Socrates cites many passages from the *Iliad* and the *Odyssey* that would not be permitted. Further constraints will be put on literature to discourage laughter and lying and encourage self-restraint.

Analysis

Socrates' critique of Homer as a bad influence becomes even clearer in this book, which provides numerous quotes that show (to Plato) how Homer has misguided Greek's beliefs. While Plato's heretical implications can be dismissed today, his censorship would do much to ruin the very aspects that have made Homer's works timeless literary works.

Later in the *Republic*, Socrates will replace this foundation of Greek society with a new myth, one that unifies rather than divides society.

2. Proper Forms of Music and Poetry
(392c–403c)

Summary

While constraints on the representation of heroes and gods are easily produced, it is more difficult to define how the poets should deal with men, given that justice has not yet been defined. At present, poets use descriptions of justice similar to those presented by Glaucon, Adeimantus, and Thrasymachus. Socrates says that poets must instead praise justice.

In order to describe what type of poetry is permissible for the Guardians to read aloud, Socrates distinguishes between imitation [alternate translation representation], which is the direct address of a character, and simple narrative, which is when the poet speaks as himself. Because the Guardians are only to aim at one kind of excellence, they will not be allowed to read the words of any person or thing that is unlike themselves—especially if it is a person who is unheroic. For this reason, only poetry that is primarily narrative will be allowed, and any poet or actor who specializes in representation will be banned from the city.

For music, only the kinds that are suitable for the depiction of "moderate and courageous men" wil be allowed (399c). This will result in a reduction of permissible musical instruments and rythms. Other arts and crafts will be similarly limited to the depiction of what is good. Ultimately, this state of education will teach a man to love beauty and hate ugliness instinctively, which will in later life lead him to love reason.

In loving relations between older and younger men, only the affection appropriate to a son may be expressed. Sexual desires must be controlled.

Analysis

Socrates' prior assertion that a man should only practice one trade forms a weak base for his desire to keep the Guardians from reciting the words of characters who do not behave in a Guardian-like fashion. Socrates supports his elimination of the representation of nonideal types by saying that a man can only represent one kind of character well. This argument is a poor one, since a good actor

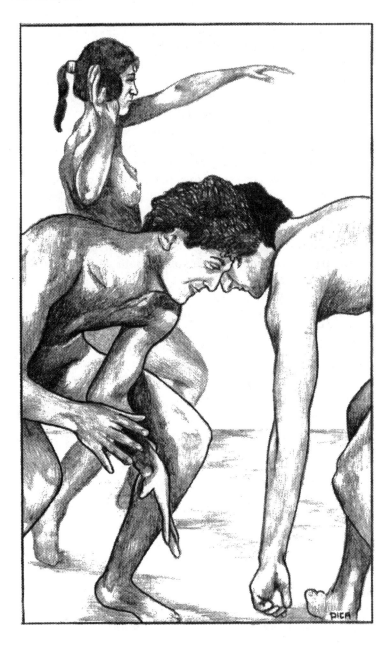

is known for his range, and both Plato and Socrates must have seen actors who performed varied roles well.

A stronger argument, which parallels modern ones used against violence in entertainment, is that having the Guardians recite these speeches will constitute their modeling themselves after these bad characters. Socrates further claims (at 401c) that living among representations of bad things has a cumulative negative effect on the soul. These arguments, like modern ones, are based on logic, not on empirical evidence.

Socrates' remarks on the proper nature of loving relations between men should not be ignored. Homosexual relations between men were celebrated in Greek society. The most common form was one in which an older man served as a mentor to a younger man; it is referred to in asides throughout the *Republic*. The older man was often besotted with the charms of the youth, while the younger man was more emotionally reserved.

Plato did not approve of the sexual nature of these pederastic relations, although he does not question the concept of passionate love between men. Given women's lack of education, it is perhaps unsurprising that Greek men believed true love could only exist within their own gender. (For more information, see Plato's *Symposium* or the second volume of Michel Foucault's *History of Sexuality*.)

3. Physical Education (403c–412a)

Summary

Food, like music, must be simple. The Guardians should eat food that is appropriate for soldiers; Socrates draws upon Homer's descriptions to illustrate the proper sorts of dishes.

Modern life has softened people. Because of the general good health of the Guardians, only medicine aimed at curing a specific illness will be practiced or needed. Those who are in bad health will be allowed to die.

Music and physical training are necessary and complementary elements of education. The man who mixes both in their proper ratios can be called "well-harmonized," because he has properly blended bravery with orderliness and tameness. This sort of person should be in charge of the state.

Analysis

In this passage Plato constructs an interesting comparison between judges and doctors. While both work for the health of the state, an excess of either shows that a state is in poor health. (Plato is clearly referring to the condition of Athens.) Both professions are supposed to deal with their patients in a way that will keep the state in good health. The good doctor will therefore allow the sickly to die, so that they don't produce unhealthy children; and those who have a bad nature will be killed by the state, presumably for similar reasons (410). This reveals the predeliction for eugenics that Plato will display more thoroughly in Book Five, when he examines reproduction in the ideal state.

4. The Three Social Classes and the Noble Lie (412b–415d)

Summary

Socrates turns to the matter of choosing leaders for his state. The highest class will be the Guardians, who will identify with the community and always aim to promote its interests. They would be rigorously tested in youth to cull out those who might fall away from the virtues their education has attempted to inculcate in them. Socrates then splits the Guardians in two. Those who pass the tests will be the Rulers (and are also still called the Guardians). Those who have not passed the tests will be Auxiliaries.

In order to unify society, Socrates proposes the creation of a new myth. This "noble lie" will teach that all of the members of the community are brothers, born of Mother Earth and forged within her womb. Some were forged with gold in them, some with silver, and the rest with bronze. The metal within each determines his place in society; those with gold are the Rulers, those with silver are Auxiliaries, and the others are the laboring class.

Because the people all come of the same stock, a child will occasionally be born into the wrong class. The Rulers must there-

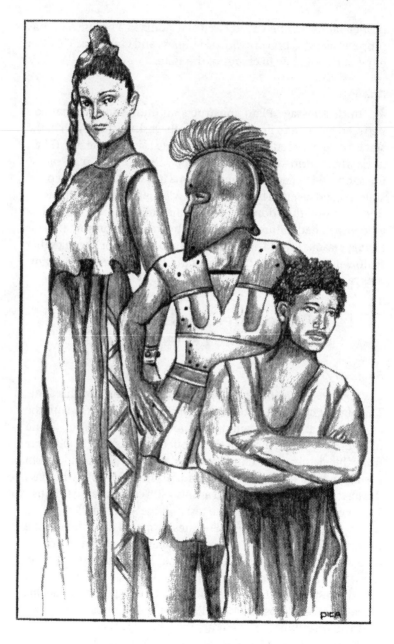

fore vigilantly evaluate the nature of each child, moving any who is of a different metal than its parents to its appropriate class. Finally, the myth will hold that the state will be destroyed when a bronze or silver man is a Guardian.

Glaucon says that it is not likely that people will believe this myth at first, although he thinks they will in time.

Analysis

Plato's "noble lie" is a profound critique of Athenian democracy as well as the values of the Athenians. Athenians did not act as if their fellow citizens were their brothers; the politics of Athens was highly divisive and looked too often at individual or class interest—not at what would be best for all of society.

Karl Popper and others find this passage indicative of Plato's totalitarian tendencies. This charge is countered by Desmond Lee, who finds part of the problem in the translation "noble lie," which he interprets as "magnificent myth." Lee says it is unfair to charge Plato with encouraging "manipulation by propaganda"; after all, the myth is intended for the consumption of all of the classes (Lee, 1974: 177).

While the noble lie's assertion of inherent inequality is difficult to swallow, it is easier to appreciate the value of having a society unified at such a fundamental level. The *Iliad* had obviously provided a common identity among Greeks, but Plato felt that it had come at too high a price, producing a people who devalued justice, accepted selfishness, and ignored a variety of other ills. Plato is therefore attempting to cure the ills of Athens by going directly to the origin of its problem. Mere tinkering with laws is no longer a viable method to create a good state.

5. Lifestyle of the Guardians (415e–417d)

Summary

Socrates asserts that the Guardians must lead a lifestlye that will enable them to do their duties while keeping them from harming the community. He therefore proposes the Guardians have no private property and that they live and eat together like soldiers do in camp. They will receive food as wages for services provided from the members of the community. They will be forbidden to touch gold or silver. While they will be told that this is for fear of contaminating the gold within them, in actuality it is to keep them from becoming tyrants.

Analysis

Overall, Socrates' recommendations for the lifestyle of the Guardians parallels the lifestyle of the Spartans, Athens' rival. The Spartans' lives were lived in continuous military service, and many contemporary Greeks admired their singleminded devotion to their state. Plato certainly appreciated many elements of the Spartan lifestyle, but he found certain areas deficient.

One of these was the Spartan system of helotry. The helots were the slaves who worked the Spartans' land. They were frequently abused, even hunted, by their overlords. The helots frequently rose in revolt; and it was primarily for this reason that the Spartans were forced to be continually ready for war (Finley, 1964). Plato radically restructures the relations between the classes in his ideal state by unifying them and replacing class interests with the happiness of all.

Spartans were also famed for their stupidity, mocked memorably in Aristophanes' *Lysistrata*. Plato attempts to soften this element through his encouragement of music and philosophy, which he finds necessary to soften the aggressiveness caused by the Spartan emphasis on strictly military virtues. Yet Plato does not criticize Spartans' resistance to change; instead, he insists on a rigid adherence to the beliefs and practices and, most especially, the education he has described. In the real world, it was this very "mental inflexibility," according to M. I. Finley, that brought Sparta down after so much success (Finley, 1964: 86).

Study Questions

1. Why would Socrates censor the passage in the *Iliad* that refers to a soul "bewailing his fate, leaving manliness and the bloom of youth"?

2. What does Socrates predict will be the result of a citizen lying?

3. What sort of dramatic role will the Guardians be permitted to play?

4. Why does Socrates say eliminating the use of musical instruments helps improve the state?

5. What can rythm and harmony do for the mind when properly absorbed?

6. What profession grows when the citizens of a city are poorly disciplined?

7. How does an obsession with one's health interfere with the practice of philosophy?

8. What two things must a man bring into harmony within himself?

9. What is the purpose of the "noble lie"?

10. Why must the Guardians not be allowed private property?

Answers

1. This passage from the *Iliad* would teach children to fear death, interfering with their ability to be good warriors.

2. If anyone in the state besides the rulers tells lies, he will be punished for introducing a practice that will likely ruin the state.

3. The Guardians will be allowed to play the role of men of good characters, especially when they act "steadily and prudently" (396d).

4. Socrates says that eliminating superfluous musical instruments will help rid the state of luxury.

5. Rythm and harmony teach the mind grace and beauty.

6. A lack of discipline within the city results in an increase in lawyers (and/or judges).

7. When one is always worried about one's health, the small changes one notices will be seen as the results of one's philosophical studies.

8. A man must seek to harmonize his spirited (or energetic) side with his philosophic side.

9. The purpose of the "noble lie" is to unify the members of society.

10. The Guardians must not be allowed private property for fear it will turn them into tyrants by distracting them from focusing on the good of the state.

Suggested Essay Topics

1. Contrast Socrates' description of the *Iliad*'s influence on Athenian values with the values he wishes to teach. Which values does he not discuss that are important to a good state? Why are these values important?

2. Why does Socrates criticize an excess of lawsuits? How does legal activity reflect the health of the state, in your opinion?

Book Four

1. Happiness of the Guardians (419–421c)

Summary

Adeimantus questions whether or not the Guardians will be happy, as they will possess none of those things that are "conventionally held to belong to men who are going to be blessed" (419a).

Socrates responds that, while the Guardians will likely be happy, the goal has been the happiness of the whole city. The conventional definition of happiness as wealth would make craftsmen poor at their crafts. It would be far worse for the Guardians to be corrupted in such a way, for if they fail at their task the city will be destroyed.

Analysis

Most interesting in this passage is the references it makes to Socrates' trial. Adeimantus asks Socrates for his *apology*—or defense—against the accusations he lists. These courtroom terms, according to Allan Bloom, remind us that Socrates' way of thinking was thought to be injurious to the state. "[F]rom the various instances in which he is forced to make an *apology*, one can piece together the true reasons for Socrates', and hence the philosopher's, conflict with the city...[E]very use of this word casts an ominous shadow." (Bloom, 1991: 455)

2. Maintenance of Unity (421d–427c)

Summary

Socrates says that to keep the city at its best, it is necessary for the Guardians to keep wealth and poverty out of the city. The city will easily be able to defend itself against rich opponents. As long as the city keeps to its program for education, it will stay unified and devoted to keeping all things in common.

Socrates declines to enter into specifics on laws regarding contracts, manners, and religion. While he expects religious matters to be determined by the temple of Apollo at Delphi and manners to emerge smoothly from the well-educated citizens, he dismisses the possibility of difficulties in determining the specifics of regulatory law within his ideal state. If the society finds itself constantly changing the law, it will be a sign that the society has fallen away from health. In this situation the person who tells a society what its members need to do to solve their problems will be seen as "the greatest enemy of all" (426a).

Analysis

In this section, Plato once again inserts references to Socrates' life. Socrates proclaimed that fundamental changes were needed to restore Athens to health, and his reward was execution. Plato is bitter that Athens continues to bestow blessings on those who (in his opinion) only flatter it. Since these men will not prescribe the bitter medicine that is necessary to cure Athens' ills, Plato sees them as false statemen.

This passage also incorporates the "doctrine of the mean"—"mean" in this case meaning average. Rather than praising extremes, such as unlimited wealth, the doctrine of the mean prefers the middle. This is the philosophy behind Socrates' rejection of both wealth and poverty, which leads him to have the Guardians guard against both of these extremes. Both moderns and Athenians might find Socrates' critique of wealth poorly constucted, but the abstract form of the argument, of avoiding extremes, seems sensible.

3. Justice in the State (427d–434d)

Summary

Socrates says that the city he has described is perfect and possesses the virtues of wisdom, courage, moderation (alt. trans. "self-discipline"), and justice. The Guardians, though few, have imparted their wisdom to the city. The soldiers, who will preserve what they have been taught to believe fearful, provide its courage. Insofar as the well-educated element of the city controls the base desires of the masses and all of the elements of the city agree that the best-educated element should rule, the city is self-disciplined. Because the members of the city don't interfere in each other's business or possessions, the city is just.

Analysis

Socrates initially constructed a hypothetical city to enable the reader to see justice writ large. Now he is preparing for a return to the initial problem of justice in the individual. After finding three of the "four cardinal virtues" in his city, he determines that the final one, justice, must also be present. He finds that it is, insofar as the city has each man performing the activities at which he is best, which he defined as a just arrangement in Book Two. Since relation of the classes in his city has produced justice, Socrates will now analogize this arrangement to the proper one for the soul of an individual.

4. Conflict in the Individual (434e–441c)

Summary

Socrates attempts to determine if the mind is made of one part or many. Moving from the assumption that one object cannot perform two opposite functions at the same time, he finds that the mind, which can have a desire and yet control it, must have at least two parts. He defines these first two parts as appetite and reason. He also discovers the existence of a third element, called spirit, which he finds usually sides with reason.

Analysis

By deciding upon three constituent elements of the mind, Socrates is now ready to find each equivalent to an element of the city in speech. The existence of a proper relation between each will therefore mean that justice exists in the individual.

Plato's division of the mind is often called his doctrine of the three parts of the soul. Desmond Lee notes that Plato also follows this doctrine in the *Phaedrus* and *Timaeus*, although he uses a unified theory in the *Symposium* (Lee, 1974: 207).

5. Justice Within the Individual (441d–444)

Summary

Socrates draws parallels between reason and the Guardians, spirit and the Auxiliaries, and appetite and the masses. The similarity between the three elements of the personality and of the state lead Socrates to say that the individual will be just when the three elements of the personality stay in their proper role, with reason ruling and the other elements subordinate to it. He determines that justice really is concerned with what is within: the just man "sets his own house in order and rules himself" (443d). Injustice occurs when the elements of personality are not in their proper relationship.

Analysis

In this passage, Socrates likens the mind to the city in speech. He follows this with a medical analogy; good mental health is similar to good physical health insofar as good actions produce good results in both. Both of these analogies are strained, but they allow Socrates to make the point that justice is concerned with the mind, not with the exterior world and its benefits, thereby meeting Adeimantus' request from Book Two—that is, to compare justice with injustice not by virtue of its material benefits, but by virtue of its positive effect on a man's soul.

6. Conclusion and Transition
to the State (445)

Summary

Socrates, attempting to turn to the question of the worth of justice, is interrupted by Glaucon. Glaucon says that it is clear that a man would prefer a life of justice, because it would be as ridiculous to choose injustice as it would be for a man to deliberately choose illness over health.

Socrates then starts a discussion of the different forms of imperfect states, which fall into four noteworthy types. Since each type of state is parallelled by a personality, he aims to describe five of each (including the ideal). The regime he has been describing is the type that would be called either a kingship or an aristocracy, depending upon how many exceptional men were involved in its rule.

Analysis

This section is a brief preface to the description of the different types of regimes and personalities that Socrates will give in Book Eight. The health analogy appears again in this section.

Study Questions

1. What four virtues will the ideal state possess?

2. Whose happiness does the ideal state seek?

3. How does the "doctrine of the mean" explain Socrates' desire to keep the city's workmen from becoming rich?

4. Why does Socrates not fear his city falling in war?

5. What metaphor describes the well-regulated state as well as the well-ordered mind?

6. What three elements compose the mind?

7. Who is allowed to rule in the ideal state?

8. What class does "appetite" correspond to?

9. What two forms of rule does Socrates find appropriate to the ideal state?

10. What would be the worst thing to happen within the ideal state?

Answers

1. The ideal state will possess wisdom, courage, moderation (or self-discipline), and justice.

2. The ideal state seeks the happiness of all.

3. Socrates wishes to avoid extremes, so he prefers that workmen be neither rich nor poor.

4. Because the state will not be rich, Socrates predicts it will easily defeat lazy states and will easily find allies if it should seek them.

5. The well-regulated state and the well-regulated mind are both in good health.

6. The mind is composed of reason, spirit, and appetite.

7. Only the Guardians, who have gold within them, will be allowed to rule.

8. The working classes correspond to the mental element of appetite.

9. Socrates says the ideal state will either be ruled as an aristocracy or as a kingship.

10. The worst thing to happen within the ideal state would be for a member of the silver or bronze classes to get into the Guardians.

Suggested Essay Topics

1. Explain Socrates' justification of the limitation of the activities of the members of the state. How does this relate to justice in the individual? Does this argument work in both cases?

2. Contrast the function of happiness in a free-market society with that of happiness in the city in speech. Does happiness have a value in the state, and, if so, what is it?

SECTION SIX

Book Five

1. The Position of Women (451d–457b)

Summary

Adeimantus asks Socrates to elaborate about the community of wives and children which he had briefly mentioned earlier. Referring to the previous analogies to watchdogs, Socrates asserts that the women in society should be trained and expected to perform the same duties as the men. Women and men are not of different natures, so women are capable of performing every occupation. Therefore, having women serve as Guardians is quite natural, as it is among the many things at which they may excel. Men will naturally be better than women at every task as well as being stronger; but training the women in this way will result in the state producing "the best possible women and men" (457e).

Analysis

This is a highly disputed passage. Its references to the playwright Aristophanes, who parodied women's equality in his *Ecclesiazusae*—as well as Socrates in the *Clouds*—are clear, but how serious Plato is about women's equality is not.

Desmond Lee says that the concept of women's equality was "in the air" before the *Republic* was written, which is why Aristophanes was inspired to parody them in the *Ecclesiazusae* (Lee, 1974:225). In contrast, Allan Bloom says that the idea that women could lead the same sort of life as men had not previously existed

"in the thoughts of serious men" (Bloom, 1991:380). By discussing it, Plato is attempting to beat Aristophanes at his own game: comedy. Bloom strongly supports his argument against Plato's seriousness. He says that since Socrates argues that "the best women are always inferior to the best men," it would be "highly improbable that any woman would even be considered for membership in the higher classes."

While this follows from Plato's argument, eliminating women from the Guardian classes would make his later recommendation for the abolition of the family impossible to achieve. The common Greek would doubtlessly have found the concept of women's equality humorous; but Plato's argument is quite sound. To achieve similar virtues, one must provide a similar education to both sexes. It is interesting to note that the debate about women's involvement in the military has continued in this more egalitarian era.

2. Reproduction and Child Raising (457c–461e)

Summary

Socrates asserts that, following his previous arguments, men and women shall not be allowed to form households, and traditional parent-child relationships must be abolished. Instead, women and children will be held in common by all.

Much as owners breed only their best animals together, so must the rulers aim to see that the best members of the Guardians breed as frequently as possible. To keep arguments from arising within the Guardian class, the rulers will have to "use a throng of lies and deceptions" about the nature of these practices, making sure that it seems that they occur through chance. These deceptions are all justified because they work to the "benefit of the ruled." (459d)

After the children are born, the well-bred ones will be raised in a nursery, while the poorly-bred ones will be hidden away "in an unspeakable place" (460a). The parents will not be allowed to know who their children are, and children will not know their parents. To guard against incest, an artificial system of familial relations

will be established. This should ensure that parents do not breed with their children, but its breadth will also cause the state to be even more unified.

Analysis

In this passage, Plato's advocation of eugenics is laid out most clearly. This practice, which had a worldwide revival after Darwin's *Origin of Species* was published, was finally discredited after its evil implications were brought to fruitition in Nazi Germany.

Plato is especially criticized (by Karl Popper) for advocating infanticide. However, the Greeks saw "nothing very shocking" in this concept, according to Desmoned Lee. Sparta routinely exposed defective children, and illegitimate ones often met the same fate in Athens. Plato is somewhat vague on the topic, however; Lee ascribes this to his "basic dislike of killing" (Lee, 1974: 246).

3. Movement Between Classes (462–466d)

Summary

Socrates argues that his city has done the most to foster unity and community among its members. The people strongly identify with their community and are dedicated to the common good. The Guardians will experience none of the dissension caused by private property or private feelings. The society will be at peace with itself. Socrates concludes that the Guardians will truly be happy.

Analysis

Allan Bloom proposes that the entire purpose of the reconstruction of familial relations is to move these ties from a small group to the whole city. While the ties thus established would certainly be weaker than blood ties, the elimination of loyalty to the smaller family group would certainly have a substantial impact on the operation of a state.

Plato's attempt to eliminate completely the biological family constitutes a historically radical change in the organization of human relationships. It is unsurprising that even Plato's student Aristotle believed it impossible. Whether or not Plato thought it could work, it is important to keep in mind what problems he thought this action would solve, as well as how it reflects his understanding of what a family was outside of the biological context.

4. Regulating Warfare (466e–471e)

Summary

Socrates would have men and women warring together, taking the children with them when they are old enough. Measures would be taken to ensure the children's safety, including keeping them on horses so they can flee if necessary. Brave warriors would be greatly honored. The dead would be buried with great ceremony and worshipped as guardian spirits.

Socrates and Glaucon agree that it is a bad practice to enslave conquered Greeks, which could allow barbarians to conquer Greece. Greeks should fight barbarians and leave one another alone. Socrates asserts that it is natural for Greeks to war against barbarians, because they are different from each other and are enemies by nature; but Greeks are kin to each other, and fighting among them is unnatural—a sign that "Greece is sick" (470c).

Since Greeks are naturally friends, warfare must be moderated between them, keeping in mind the reconciliation that they should aim for. This means no more destroying land or houses. Glaucon agrees, adding "toward the barbarians they must behave as the Greeks do now toward one another." (471b)

Analysis

This passage strongly shows the sense of identity the Hellenes shared. Plato has implicitly accepted that warfare is a natural state, but he feels that the Greeks must overcome their petty differences. Plato's pleas for unity were unfortunately not heeded. The historical fall of Athens makes these writings especially poignant.

5. Introduction to the Philosopher-King
(471c–474b)

Summary

Glaucon praises the advantages of the ideal state Socrates has been describing, but questions whether or not it is possible. Socrates reminds Glaucon that this purpose has been only to establish what the ideal is, not to prove if it is possible to achieve it. Ideals are necessary to provide standards against which to measure one's closeness to perfection. However, to approach the perfection of the city of speech, one change in current practice would do the most: philosophers must "rule as kings"—or kings must learn philosophy (474b).

Analysis

Many of the practical problems of Socrates' ideal state are swept away with his pronouncement that he has only been establishing an ideal (except, of course, for the question of whether or not this constitutes an ideal). Plato chooses at this point to focus on an element that he believes is practical—the establishment of philosopher-kings.

Plato was quite serious about this proposal. His trips to the court of Dionysius of Syracuse were an attempt to put his theories into practice with an actual monarch. While he failed with Dionysius, his later involvement with Hermias of Atarneus resulted in the melioration of what had previously been tyrannical rule (Lee, 1974:20).

6. Definition of the Philosopher
(474c–480)

Summary

Socrates says he must first define what a philosopher is. This will enable him to show that some people are naturally suited to philosophy and leadership, while all others should instead follow the leader.

In order to be a philosopher, a man must love every sort of learning. Philosophers seek to learn the truth that lies behind the world of the senses. This world of absolutes, of pure beauty or justice (for example), exists in a realm that can only be apprehended through the exercise of reason. (This is the realm of "forms" or "ideas.") He who knows this world has knowledge; he who only knows things in the everyday world has opinions.

Socrates criticizes those who claim to love wisdom but deny that "forms" exist. Things in the real world cannot be defined in an absolute sense and will change when compared to something else. This is the reason why people who claim to love wisdom but look only at the real world have only opinions and not knowledge.

Analysis

Plato's theory of forms may be difficult to grasp at first. To understand the concept, imagine looking at a rather large, soft, flat piece of furniture. During the moment of uncertainty about this object's name, you would compare it to the "forms" or "ideas" of different types of furniture in your head, finally concluding it was a bed.

Just as there are many types of beds in the real world (round, low, large, etc.) and only one "form" of a bed in your head, so are there many different definitions of more abstract concepts (such as beauty, justice, happiness, etc.) but only one "form" of each. To Plato, an absolute definition of any of these things can only exist in reference to the world of forms.

For a further explanation of this topic, see Lee, 1974:263-267.

Study Questions

1. What will be women's role in the Guardian class?

2. How will Guardian women be involved in raising their children?

3. What guide do the Rulers follow in arranging the breeding of their fellow citizens?

4. What simple change would make the improvements of the city in speech a possibility in the real world?

5. What faculty enables one to perceive the world of forms?

6. What does a person "know" who denies the existence of the world of forms?

7. Why does Socrates say warfare between the Greeks should be more limited than it was?

8. What third realm lies below the world of opinion?

9. What will the female Guardians wear when they exercise?

10. How will family ties continue in the ideal state?

Answers

1. Women will be educated and perform the same tasks as the men, although the men will be better at everything.

2. Guardian women will go to the nurseries to feed the children when they are nursing, but they will not know which child is theirs.

3. The Rulers want to make sure that they encourage the breeding of the best citizens.

4. Socrates says that the institution of philosopher-kings would do much to improve the way states are ruled.

5. It is through reason that one comes to know the world of forms.

6. A person who does not know the world of forms can only have opinions, not knowledge.

7. Socrates says that the Greeks are naturally friends and should fight each other in a more civilized fashion.

8. The realm of ignorance lies below that of opinion.

9. According to Socrates, excellence will be all the clothes they need.

10. In the ideal state, family ties will be transferred to all of the members of the community.

Suggested Essay Topics

1. How does Plato feel familial relations affect the state? What should their place be, in your opinion?

2. Is war a natural or unnatural state? How does Plato feel about this question? Substantiate Plato's view with textual support.

Book Six

1. The Philosopher's Character (484–487a)

Summary

Philosophers who have true vision are best suited to guard the laws and customs of a city. Other people are blind compared to them. Philosophers love truth, spurn physical pleasures, and don't fear death. They are temperate, courageous, and just. Philosophers also learn easily and have a good memory. Finally, philosophers' grace and sense of proportion enable them to easily understand the nature of the forms. These, then, are the people to whom the state must be entrusted.

Analysis

The description of a philosopher that Plato puts in Socrates' mouth is anything but humble. To some degree, it is designed specifically to counteract the charges of the Athenians that philosophers (especially Socrates) sought to overturn the moral foundations of the state; instead, they are depicted as the only true guardians of the laws and customs. The other aspects respond to the common Athenian belief that philosophers themselves were immoral, as summarized in the next section.

The description Socrates paints of the true philosopher is congruent with the previous description of the Guardian. The philosopher is more remarkable, however, because he acquired these noble traits without the full support of society.

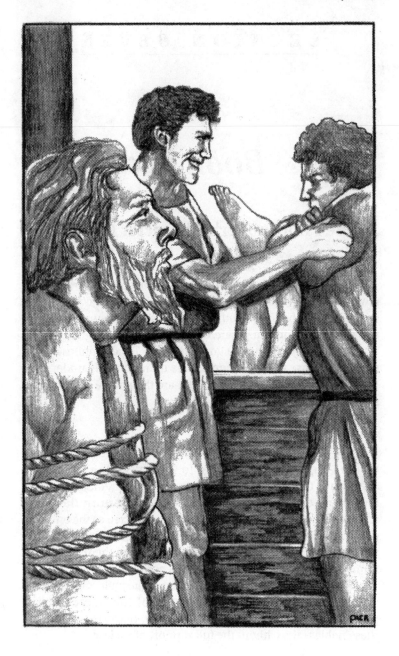

2. The Corruption of the Philosopher (487b–497a)

Summary

Adeimantus counters Socrates' description with the common view of philosophers: most of them are strange, some of them are vicious, and at best they are utterly useless.

To explain why society sees philosophers as useless, Socrates tells the parable of the ship of state. The captain (representing the people) is strong but not a good navigator because he is nearsighted. The crew (representing the politicians) fights to wrest control of the ship away from the captain, although none of them know how to navigate. Failing to convince the captain to give them the ship, the sailors overpower him with narcotics and drink and feast away.

Meanwhile, the navigator (who represents the philosopher) is condemned as useless because of the length of time needed to learn his worthless skill. The crew does not even believe that it is possible to learn navigation. For the crew, respect goes to the person who is best at controlling the captain.

Socrates agrees that philosophers are often corrupted. He blames this situation on the effect of a bad environment on a man with an excess of talent. For example, innate leadership potential attracts people who will flatter a man until he becomes insufferable and ambitious. These companions will discourage this natural philosopher from following the path of philosophy. He will eventually become vicious and harm the body politic.

Yet the worst element of the Athenian environment is the temptation to go along with the crowd, which is made even stronger by various punishments for those who offend this code. Ultimately, Athenian society makes the emergence of a truly good man nearly impossible.

Socrates condemns the Sophists as mere animal trainers. While they know how to get their animal (the public) to respond in a certain way, they fail to question the morality of the actions their animal takes. For this reason they are incapable of prescribing an action on moral grounds; they can only recommend actions that suit the public's tastes.

Philosophy suffers greatly under these conditions. While they continue, the best thing a philosopher can do is avoid politics altogether.

Analysis

Plato roundly damns Athenian political culture in this metaphor-laden passage. The public is described as a many-headed hydra, the rhetoriticians who controlled the Assembly as animal trainers, and the whole system as a misguided ship. While moderns would praise such a system for its high degree of participation, Plato instead curses it as a society that is incapable of taking the right course because it only wants to hear itself praised.

Plato's invective, while providing a good look at Athenian opinion regarding philosophy, seems also to be colored by more personal matters. First, Plato was incapable of forgiving Athens for its condemnation of Socrates; he constantly has Socrates making remarks about the dangers liable to befall a critic of the state. Yet Athens had far more freedom for criticism than Sparta did, and a work like the *Republic* could never have arisen from Spartan society. Second, it is interesting to note that one of the people who condemned philosophy as an unrealistic study for those who wished to serve in the government was Isocrates, whose school of rhetoric was in direct competition with Plato's Academy (Lee, 1974). This passage can therefore be seen as a defense of Plato's method as well as of his master.

3. The Philosopher-King: A Practical Idea (497b–502c)

Summary

Socrates claims that there is no society that is hospitable to the philosophic nature. Most people don't believe in the value of philosophy, and until the uncorrupted philosophers compel them to listen to them or until a king loves philosophy, this situation will not change.

Since the philosopher keeps his eyes on the perfect realm of the forms, he internalizes its order and divinity, which he would impart to all men if given the chance. To do so would require that the philosopher-king "wipe clean" men's dispositions and the arrangements of political society (501a). He would then completely reconstruct them according to the divine pattern. Until philosophers rule in the cities, "there will be no rest from ills either for city or citizens," and the city in speech will never come into existence (501e).

Analysis

After previously discounting the city in speech as a metaphorical ideal, Plato has contradicted himself by asserting that such a city might be possible were there a philosopher-king. He will waver back and forth between goal and ideal throughout the *Republic*. While Allan Bloom finds evidence that the city in speech is only a philosophical joke, many others have believed it to be a serious description.

It is difficult to say which view is right. Yet Plato's claim that human nature is capable of being completely remade—that it is fully a construct of society and not at all of nature—supports the claim that his city in speech is a goal he would like to achieve. Modern critiques of the possibility of Plato's proposals for the ideal state draw strongly on the "nature versus nurture" debate, claiming that Plato has overstated the case for the malleability of human society and provide historical and anthropological evidence to support these claims. Whether or not he was serious, it is generally agreed that the city in speech is not possible.

4. Theory of Forms: Sun Simile (502d–509c)

Summary

Socrates says that the Guardians must be philosophers. Because it takes so many conflicting qualities to be a good Guardian, their numbers will be few, and those eligible to go on to philosophy will be even fewer. This tiny group will advance through higher intellectual studies as they age in preparation for the greatest study: the form of the Good. Knowledge of the Good is necessary so that people may deliberately "do, possess, and enjoy" what is truly good instead of what has been mistakenly thought to be good (505d). This is especially true for the Rulers, who must guide the city toward the Good.

To explain the Good, Socrates uses the simile of the sun. In order to see an object, the eye needs the sun to illuminate the object. For the mind to "see" (intellectually) a form, it needs the form of the Good to provide the lesser form illumination. As the sun produces growth and light, so does the Good produce reality and truth. Forms illuminated by the Good are easy to see.

Analysis

Plato's simile is somewhat obscure in these days of sonar and incandescent bulbs. Yet the basic idea, that the Good is the primary form, the one whose radiance makes all of the other elements of this realm visible, is clear enough. A more modern simile focusing on proof of the existence of the Good might be to compare it to a black hole. Astronomers, of course, cannot see black holes, but they can see their effects on other heavenly bodies. These effects provide indirect proof that black holes exist, allowing astronomers to study black holes. Plato wishes philosophers to make similar attempts to study the Good.

5. Theory of Forms Continued: The Divided Line (509d–511)

Summary

Continuing his discussion of the sun and the form of the Good, Socrates portrays each as king of a realm: the sun of the visible realm, the Good to the realm of forms (the intelligible realm). Much as the visible realm can be divided into images (such as shadows and reflections) and the objects that produce them, the intelligible realm can be divided into a section of pure philosophy and a lower section that is involved with the logical interpretation of the visible world.

Glaucon says he interprets Socrates' argument as showing that philosophy is a higher form of reason than math and the sciences, which are locked into the world of the senses. Socrates agrees, naming a hierarchy of states of mind corresponding to each of the four segments of the line: intelligence to the top, then reason, followed by belief (which is in the realm of the senses), and finally by illusion (or imagination). On this scale, these states of mind reflect the degree of truth in the subject matter they examine, with intelligence examining objects of pure truth, and illusion examining purely imaginary objects.

Analysis

To make the case for the rule of philosophers, Plato must show that theirs is a superior form of knowledge. He sets up dialectic—intellectual investigation via dialogue—as the only way of acquiring true knowledge about the subjects that he claims lie behind proper rule. Since those who engage in mathematics or rhetoric can never understand what the Good is, their rule could never result in the production of a just state. In the modern world, his argument would also suffice against rule by technicians, who may apply scientific procedures to determine proper rule, but who are limited by an inability to look at the moral consequences of their actions.

Unfortunately, Plato's argument is undermined by his insistence on the actual existence of forms. As an intellectual construct, the realm of forms makes sense, but the idea that the definitions of these forms is absolute and not also influenced by culture is questionable at best. Nonetheless, Plato's push to keep politics focused on what is good instead of what is popular is still valid, especially in an age in which statecraft has become merely the outcome of opinion polls.

Study Questions

1. Why is the study of math inferior to that of philosophy?
2. What "state of mind" deals with reflections of objects?
3. How is the Good's role in the world of forms like that of the sun's in relationship to plants?
4. How does the Good help one see objects in the realm of forms?
5. What is the highest form of knowledge?

6. What one change could help bring an end to the illnesses of states?

7. Who does the navigator represent in the parable of the ship of state?

8. What is the strong animal referred to at line 493?

9. What is the problem with the way "animal trainers" handle this animal?

10. What will be the first action of the philosopher-king?

Answers

1. Math is an inferior study because, although it uses logic, it applies it to the realm of the senses.

2. Imagination is the state of mind that deals with reflections of objects.

3. The Good is the cause of the forms, although it does not take part in the process that creates them.

4. The Good casts the light of reality and truth on the objects within the realm of forms.

5. Knowledge of the Good is the highest form of knowledge.

6. Instituting rule by philosopher-kings would do the most to cure the illnesses of states.

7. The navigator represents the philosopher.

8. The strong animal is the public.

9. Animal trainers do not consider if the action they can make an animal perform is right or wrong.

10. The first action of the philosopher-king will be to wipe clean the slate of human society.

Suggested Essay Topics

1. Plato asserts that the rule of the philosopher-king will be good. What problems do you see in his argument?

2. What is Plato's opinion of the common man? How does this reflect his view on equality?

Book Seven

1. The Allegory of the Cave (514–521b)

Summary

Socrates continues his indirect description of the Good with his allegory of the cave. In the cave, men live shackled to the wall, only capable of staring straight ahead. All they can see are the shadows of images carried between a curtain and a fire by some other people, who talk and make noises. The prisoners assume that what they see and hear is reality.

If a man were released and forced outside, the brilliance would be painful and make everything difficult for him to understand. Socrates says the man would prefer the cave, but as his eyes acclimated he would realize that he had been living a life of illusion in a world where he never even realized the sun existed. He might, out of pity, return to the cave to try to enlighten his former fellows, but if he attempted to release them to experience what they would see as madness, they would try to kill him.

Socrates says that this allegory explains why philosophers are so often mocked by society; they have been blinded by the truth of the Good, and those to whom they try to explain themselves find their ideas incomprehensible. These people are trapped in the illusory world of the senses just as much as the prisoners were trapped in the cave.

Socrates believed the ability to perceive the world of forms "is in the soul of each" (518c), requiring only a proper education to be

released. The rulers of the city must receive this education and then return from their studies to care for the city. Without their rule, the city will be "governed by men who fight over shadows with one another and form factions for the sake of ruling, as though it were some great goal" (520c). Fighting over ruling leads to the destruction of the city. The philosophers will therefore feel obligated to repay their debt to the city that raised them by ruling it properly.

Analysis

Of all the passages in the *Republic*, the allegory of the cave is the most famous. Its story of the intellectual's search for truth and the rejection of his vision by society has touched centuries of artists and philosophers alike. In modern times, the parallels between the shadow-puppet screen and television lead people to wonder if they are living in a world of illusion. The image remains remarkably fresh.

Despite its age, the meaning of this allegory continues to be vigorously debated. Allan Bloom says it is a metaphor for the relation of the philosophic soul to the city. The "horizons of law and convention" hold everyone back from the journey of knowledge (Bloom, 1991:402). Bloom concludes that Plato uses this section to show that the good city is a failure because making a philosopher rule goes against his self-interest.

According to Rex Warner, Plato is trying to teach the reader the importance of "progressive philosophical enlightenment." Unless one attempts to undergo these studies, there will be "no hope of bringing order into a distracted world" (Warner, 1958:77).

While Plato's allegory is clearly intended to further differentiate the world of the senses from the world of the forms, the story presents a more hostile attitude toward the "real" world than the earlier similes of the line and sun. Plato's frustration with the political society of Athens is almost overwhelming; he depicts its citizens as not just nearsighted, but violently determined to ignore the ridiculous situation in which they live. Even given his often hopeful comments about the common man's abilities, Plato seems to have given up all hope for the reformation of Athens.

An alternate argument could be made that Plato himself, by insisting on the superiority of the world of the forms, is just as guilty of living a life of delusions as Athens. Yet his attempts to reform tyrants and his formation of the Academy show that he was attempting to make progress in the real world. These actions show that he was following the program he advocated, of bringing the light of the truth into the cave, although he did not attempt to do it as a ruler.

2. Education of the Philosopher-King: Goals (521c–524d)

Summary

Socrates considers what type of education will lead the mind up the scale of reality to philosophy. Glaucon notes that the literary and musical education previously described was insufficient. Socrates decides to teach math, because of its relation to the real world. Yet it must be more than simple arithmetic; in order to properly develop reason, it must involve comparisons, so as to lead the mind to the understanding of qualities.

Analysis

Plato has already described the differing levels of reality in his analogy of the divided line. To draw a person up to philosophy, which is part of the section of the line devoted to knowledge, it seems only practical to use mathmatical studies, which are more accessible than philosophy.

3. Math and Astronomy (524e–531d)

Summary

Because of its ability to lead the mind toward higher truths as well as its practicality, Socrates recommends his future philosopher-kings develop their intellectual capacities with arithmetic.

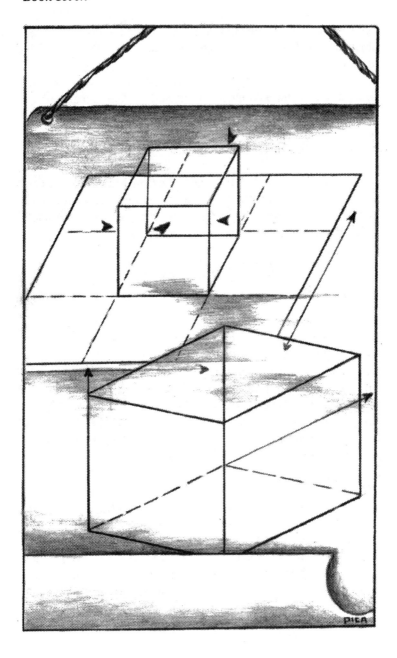

Plane geometry will be studied because of its focus on abstract objects. Solid geometry, although still in development, will also be pursued.

Although astronomy suffers from the tendency to focus on what can be seen, its ability to represent mathematical truths is very valuable. For this reason, astronomy—and harmony—will be part of the education of potential philosopher-kings.

Analysis

Socrates' description of these subjects provides a snapshot of Greek scientific inquiry at the time the *Republic* was written. Solid geometry and astronomy were just in their infancy. Of course, Plato only values these sciences as a stepping-stone to philosophy.

4. Dialectic (531c–534)

Summary

Socrates asserts that dialectic is a skill beyond that taught by the previous studies. It requires an ability to argue an idea, to try to understand an object from a purely intellectual standpoint. Other subjects fail to reach reality because they cannot surpass the limits of their assumptions.

A man must be able to define the Good and defend his definition against others' attacks, referring only to logic in his defense. If he can't do so, he is living in a world of dreams. Dialectic is therefore necessary to Socrates' city so that its rulers can rule with authority.

Analysis

According to Desmond Lee, the purpose of this passage is to differentiate the "relative reliability of different methods of perception and argument" (Lee, 1974:545). Pure thought is more reliable than reason, and the realm of knowledge is superior to the realm of opinion. He cautions against spending too much time working out a precise mathematical description of the proportion of truth in each of these segments.

5. Conclusion of the Education of the Philosopher-King (535a–541b)

Summary

Socrates describes the kind of men who are suitable for philosophic studies. They must be willing to undergo mental rigors, including actively ridding themselves of false beliefs. Socrates defines the proper ages at which each type of study should be undertaken. The students must be carefully monitored at each step to make sure only the best proceed, that their intellectual maturity is taken into account, and that the respect for authority is kept intact.

The men who successfully pass all of these trials will spend their lives alternately ruling and studying philosophy. They will rule only as a matter of necessity. Some of their members will be women. This society might all come to pass if political power were given to a philosopher who then sent away from the city all those over the age of ten.

Analysis

Socrates' description of the precautions necessary to choose the proper people for philosophic study make it seem that Plato thinks knowledge is a dangerous thing. He rightly predicts that the proper pursuit of philosophy will lead a person to question the values upon which society is founded, much as he does himself. Yet, it is surprising that he thinks that his philosophers will inevitably conclude that the way of life he has previously described is truly the one, best way. This makes it seem that he will need to choose less-gifted people in order to assure they will not argue among themselves about the best way to run a state.

Study Questions

1. What do the prisoners of the cave watch?
2. What is the first thing that the man who escapes from the cave can look at outside?
3. What is the response of the prisoners to the news of the man who has escaped about the world outside?

4. Why would a philosopher rule a state if he enjoys practicing philosophy so much?

5. What practical application does Socrates expect the Guardians to give their studies?

6. What activity will the best-educated Guardians spend most of their time doing?

7. What is the final object perceived by the man who escapes from the cave?

8. What are the two causes of a confused mind?

9. What will the prisoners believe to be the nature of the shadows that they watch?

10. How old would Guardians be before they were allowed to contemplate the Good?

Answers

1. The prisoners of the cave watch the shadows that objects cast upon a screen.

2. The first thing the escapee can look at is shadows and reflections of objects.

3. The prisoners believe the escapee is crazy.

4. The philosopher will rule a state out of a sense of obligation.

5. The Guardians can use the subjects they learn in war.

6. The best-educated Guardians will spend most of their time in the pursuit of philosophy.

7. The last object the escapee can see is the sun.

8. The two causes of a confused mind are a transition to a darker world or to a brighter world.

9. The prisoners will believe the shadows are reality.

10. Guardians would have to be 50 years old before they were allowed to pursue dialectic.

Suggested Essay Topics

1. Apply the allegory of the cave to modern society. What would the images be? Who would control them? What would the escapee see outside of the cave?

2. Explain Socrates' curriculum as it applies to the simile of the divided line.

Book Eight

1. Introduction to the Four Imperfect Societies and Their Characteristic Individuals (543–545c)

Summary

After recapitulating the elements of the ideal state, Socrates names the four imperfect states. The first and best is the Cretan or Spartan type (called "timarchy"); the second is oligarchy; the third, democracy; and the fourth and worst is tyranny. Socrates says that there are also five sorts of men: the best, corresponding to the aristocratic regime of the city in speech, and one for each of the degenerate regimes. Socrates describes these five men as falling on a descending scale of justice. He leaves until later the question of their varying degrees of happiness.

Analysis

Plato here establishes the pattern the rest of this book will follow: a description of a less-than-perfect state is followed by a description of the person who corresponds to this state. He will continue the previously used parallel between the city and the individual character, including the arrangement of the three elements of each, except that the arrangement will now show the origin of different social and psychological ills.

2. Timarchy (545d–550c)

Summary

The degeneration of the ideal state starts when disagreement arises within the ruling class. Using a complex mathematical formula derived from Pythagorean theory and Greek numerology, Socrates explains that the problems arise from disharmonious breeding. The resultant children are less capable than their predecessors were. Their degeneration leads to a mixing of metals, which is responsible for the rise of hatred and war within the ruling class as silver and gold personalities battle with the more materialistic iron and bronze ones.

The result of this conflict is that private property is introduced for the rulers, and the lower classes of society are enslaved. While the new society will have many of the elements of the old, it will differ in its fear of intelligence, its love of money, and its excess of ambition.

The timarchic character is initially caught between the good nature of his father and the ambition and hunger of the rest of society. He chooses to follow a middle road, allowing his spirited element to rule him. He will be competitive, somewhat ignorant, and violent toward his slaves. As he gets older he will become avaricious.

Analysis

According to Allan Bloom, Plato's description of the five regimes treats the regime as identical with the kind of men who rule. The regime determines every other political fact, including "the character of law, education, property, marriage, and the family" (Bloom, 1991:414). Bloom finds the historical descriptions historically impossible and fanciful at best. He claims that Plato chose to have the city ruled by philosophers as the ancestral city so that "the quest for wisdom [does] not appear to be in conflict with the political prejudice in favor of the ancestral" (Bloom, 1991:416).

While the city in speech was similar to Sparta, the timocratic state is identical to it. Plato acknowledges the shortcomings of Sparta in this passage; specifically, its fear of intellectuals, the undercurrent of avarice, and its abuse of the helots. This is important to remember when examining the construction of the city in speech. It is not just based on Athens' shortcomings, but Sparta's as well and many of its more obscure recommendations make sense when Sparta is kept in mind.

3. Oligarchy (550c–555b)

Summary

Socrates defines an oligarchy as a society "in which the rich rule and the poor man has no part in ruling office" (550d). This regime arises because of the hoarding of wealth that begins during the timocratic regime. As time passes, wealth becomes more valued than virtue, and the society changes from a state of honor-seeking warriors to one of money-grubbing businessmen.

Oligarchic society exacerbates the divisions between rich and poor. The rich become drones, mere consumers adding nothing to their society. If these drones become poor, they join the large criminal class that necessarily arises in an oligarchy. The government tries to restrain the criminals but can't, as it is in part to blame for their existence.

The oligarchic individual seeks only to make money, subduing all of the elements of his soul to its sway. He is disciplined as far as this one goal goes, but his lack of education gives him bad morals. Socrates finds this person to be generally ruled by his better impulses, although inferior to the well-balanced personality.

Analysis

In the Aristotelian analysis of political regimes, the two questions asked are "who rules" and "in whose interest." Plato's analysis focuses exclusively on the first question, although his best regime is designed specifically to benefit all. Aristotle praises all the regimes that aim to benefit the city, while condemning as bad the regimes that only seek to benefit those who are ruling. For him, an oligarchy is one of the three regimes that seeks only to benefit those who rule, and is accordingly classified, contrary to Plato's scheme, as a bad regime.

4. Democracy (555c–562)

Summary

The loss of self-discipline in the oligarchic state leads its citizens to borrow money, driving many of them into poverty and leading them to plot against society. The oligarchs become more usurious, and their children become lazier. The society quickly becomes ill, and the people fight each other with little provocation. When the poor overcome their opponents, a democracy is established, with civil rights and political opportunity for all.

The people in a democracy are free and have a wide variety of personalities. Socrates describes a democratic society as like "a many colored cloak decorated in all hues, [causing] this regime... to look fairest" (557c). While the lack of compulsion makes time pass sweetly and all it takes to rise to political power is to declare oneself the people's friend, Socrates condemns democratic society as anarchic, mistakenly treating all as equals.

The democratic character emerges as he lets his bad desires overwhelm his rational element. His mind is full of empty speeches and opinions, and he scorns the simple life. As he gets older, he pursues the pleasures democratically, allowing each one to rule him in its turn. His disposition varies widely, just as the disposition of his city does.

Analysis

Much as Socrates described the lowest class of the city as the one in which the desires held greatest sway, the democratic society and democratic man are both ruled by base desires. Moderns, like Greeks, praise democracy for its freedom and variety, but Socrates characterizes it as ruled by licence and anarchy. His description is a tragic one, because it shows this fairest of societies to contain the seeds of tyranny. Moderns might see the democratic society shadowed by the seeds of mass society, but the city in speech itself seems far worse. It is no more than a fascist state waiting for a dictator.

Allan Bloom notes that the language used in the description of the fight for the democratic man's soul recalls the Eleusinian mysteries. These rituals started with inductees purified before their initiation and concluded with a torch race. Both of these elements appear in this passage.

Note that it is the introduction of unnecessary pleasures that reduce the oligarchic character to the democratic. This is the same element that turned the city of pigs into a fevered state. Plato seems to indicate that another solution for the problems of the modern state—aside from introducing rule by philosopher-kings and wiping clean the slate of society—would be guarding against the importation of luxury.

5. Tyranny in the State (562–569c)

Summary

Socrates describes tyranny as arising naturally out of democracy's excessive love of freedom. This leads the democratic state into anarchy. The poor people then pick a leader whose unjust actions against the other members of society force him to seize power aggressively, initially under the guise of self-protection.

The tyrant's actions cause him to be unpopular, and his fear of assassination forces him into exile or to execute those who stand against him. He is obliged to maintain a large bodyguard and to keep the people in poverty. Ultimately, he will have no friends and will turn his people into slaves.

Analysis

Unlike its modern sense, a tyrant was not defined by the Greeks as a cruel ruler. Instead, a tyrant was a person who seized power illegitimately. A king could tyrannize his populace, but if he had risen to the throne dynastically (and hence legitimately), he was a king, not a tyrant. As Finley notes, the word tyrant "implied no judgment about his quality as a person or ruler. Individual tyrants in fact varied very much: some, like Peisastratus in Athens, reigned benevolently and well, put an end to civil war, helped solve the economic problems and advanced their cities in many ways" (Finley, 1964:40).

Thus, Thrasymachus' initial defense of the tyrant is not so heinous as it seems to moderns. Plato's critique of the tyrant, however, draws strongly on the possible elements of their rule, which later came to dominate the definition of the term. Aristotle also classified the tyrant as a bad ruler, because he ruled in his own interest, not necessarily because he had his enemies burnt alive.

Study Questions

1. What element of the timarchic society gives it its name?

2. Which desire does Socrates use as an example of an unnecessary one?

3. Of the three elements of the personality, which one rules the timarchic man?

4. What desire dominates oligarchic society?

5. What is the problem with the equality established in democratic society, according to Socrates?

6. Does Socrates think his ideal society could last forever, given the right conditions?

7. Who does Socrates say would be attracted to the multi-hued cloak of democratic society?

8. How does the timarchic regime treat the members of the lower class?

9. What metaphor does Socrates use to describe the tyrant's enslavement of his people?

10. Why does the tyrant have a large bodyguard?

Answers

1. The timarchic society gets its name from its love of honor.

2. A luxurious diet is described as an unnecessary desire.

3. The timarchic man is ruled by his spirited nature.

4. Oligarchic society is dominated by the love of gain.

5. Democratic societies incorrectly assume all men are equal.

6. No. Socrates believes all things must decay.

7. Children and women would find such garishness attractive.

8. The timarchic regime enslaves the lower classes.

9. The tyrant's enslavement of his people is like patricide.

10. He lives in constant fear of assassination.

Suggested Essay Topics

1. Examine Plato's critique of democracy. How do his complaints challenge modern norms? Which, if any, of his critiques has validity?

2. What elements of Spartan society does Plato criticize? How does he attempt to safeguard his ideal state from these evils?

Book Nine

1. The Tyrannical Individual (571–576b)

Summary

In order to explain the evolution of the tyrannical man, Socrates sub-divides the unnecessary pleasures, creating a category of anti-social pleasures. While these may exist within everyone, most people control theirs through the influence of the law and the active intervention of their power of reason. The tyrant is a mixture of lust, drunkenness, and madness, evil passions that can exist in anyone (as is revealed by one's dreams) but which the tyrant alone makes no attempt to restrain. By indulging his passions, the tyrannical man will find they grow insatiable and exhaust his funds attempting to satisfy them. He will completely lose all restraints and will commit every crime.

As more of these types are formed, they form gangs. When their numbers become great enough, the people of a state will choose the worst man among them to be ruler. The ruling tyrant will plunder the people, while his tyrannical lackeys will prove to be only fair-weather friends, leaving him when a better opportunity presents itself. The tyrannical type is perfectly unjust and the worst type of man.

Analysis

Plato describes the tyrannical sort as the kind of person no man would wish to be. He is faithless, indulges in low pleasures, and cannot be trusted. Plato's description would make it difficult for any man of honor to wish to be a tyrant. Even if Thrasymachus were still unconvinced by Socrates' argument, he would be unlikely to defend the life of a tyrant to the gathering without appearing to be a pervert.

2. Comparative Happiness of the Five Individuals (576c–588)

Summary

Socrates concludes that the tyrant is the unhappiest man, his state the worst. A tyrant's state is enslaved, poor, frightened, and miserable. The tyrant himself is the most miserable person in this state, because he lives in a condition of constant fear. While he has complete power to act arbitrarily, he lacks true freedom because he is dominated by his emotions. The philosopher-king is the happiest and his state is the best.

Glaucon agrees with Socrates' ranking of the happiness of the five men and states, adding that they also show similar degrees of excellence. Socrates then examines the lives of the five different men to determine which is most pleasant. Referring to the three elements of the mind and their pleasures, Socrates says that only the man in whom reason dominates could make a true judgment on which of the pleasures is best. This man also has the widest experience of the world's pleasures. Since the philosopher has the best judgment and the broadest experience of all, his choice of philosophy as the highest pleasure must be correct. The life of the philosopher is therefore the most pleasant.

Socrates adds that the philosopher's pleasures, because they partake of the world of forms more than they do the mortal world, are also more real than any sensual pleasures. Pursuing philosophy will lead to the best possible results.

As a postscript, Socrates notes that the tyrant's life is 729 times more miserable than that of the philosopher-king.

Analysis

Plato uses this section to respond to the claim (stated by Thrasymachus) that the tyrant is the happiest of men. As defended by Socrates, however, the argument in favor of philosophy is worthy of a sophist. Because Plato likes philosophy, he naturally decides that a philosopher is the best judge of everything, allowing no contrary argument to be presented. His theory of forms, which he asserts is an empirical truth, allows intellectual pursuits to be prioritized as more real than those concerned with the material world. These premises allow him to conclude that the philosopher's life is most pleasant of all because philosophers say it is so and because philosophers pleasures are more real, according to a philosophical definition.

It is unfortunate that Plato's argument is built upon such questionable premises. Better support is found in his description of the misery of the tyrant's life. This assertion has plenty of evidence to back it up, in historical times as well as modern.

3. Justice is Good for the Soul (588–592b)

Summary

To counter the assertion that evil actions are the best choice for a man who has a reputation for justice, Socrates says that such an assertion encourages men to let their bestial nature rule their life at the expense of their rational side. Evil actions and bad habits strengthen the bestial element and corrupt the spirited element of the soul. Injustice is therefore bad for the soul and not to be practiced in self-interest. For those who are by nature incapable of letting their divine element rule, it is best that they be ruled by someone who does.

Injustice cannot be recommended because it makes a man worse than he was. It is best for a wrongdoer to be caught and punished in order to tame the beast within him and free his soul to attain "its best nature, aquiring moderation and justice accompanied by prudence" (591b). Therefore, the intelligent man will seek to develop the power of his higher nature above anything else. He will work to maintain the proper balance in his soul. This will lead him to avoid politics unless he lives in the city of speech. However, he will recreate the harmony of this heavenly city within himself.

Analysis

Plato incorporates both musical metaphors and the analogy of the well-organized state in this passage. He adds to these a metaphor describing the parts of the soul as animals. The desiring part is a many-headed animal, much like the democratic state as described in Book Six. The poorly defined spirited element is personified as a lion, which can be tamed or can become violent. Finally, the rational part is pictured as a man. Plato gives two primary choices for their interaction: the man can rule the other two, or the other two can fight each other and rule the man. Of course, given the idealization of man, specifically rational, civilized, Greek man, it is clear which element Plato wishes the reader to support. Spartans might have chosen a man to represent their preferred "spirited" element; Cretans might have personified their most valued of the three elements (likely also the "spirited") as a bull.

Study Questions

1. How will the wise man cultivate the "many-headed animal"?
2. Which of the five characters is the happiest?
3. To which of the other two elements of the soul does spirit always ally itself?
4. With whom is the tyrannical character friends?
5. In what way are pleasures such as food and health inferior to philosophy?
6. Why is being caught good for a wrongdoer?
7. What pleasure governs the lowest of the three elements of the mind?
8. What creature personifies spirit?
9. Why does the philosopher know more about pleasure than, say, the money-grubber?

10. Is the tyrannical man happier when he is a tyrant or when he is a private citizen?

Answers

1. The wise man will cultivate its tamer elements and prevent the wilder ones from growing.

2. The philosopher-king is the happiest.

3. Spirit may be the natural ally of reason, but it will fight it as well as desire if it is not controlled.

4. The tyrant has no friends.

5. These pleasures emanate from the world of change, not from the unchanging world of forms. Their pleasures are therefore illusory.

6. It is good for a wrongdoer to be caught because it gives him an opportunity to try to improve himself.

7. The lowest element is dominated by love of gain or profit, which enable it to achieve its other pleasures.

8. A lion personifies spirit.

9. The philosopher knows the pleasures of gain as well as of knowledge, while the man who loves money knows nothing of the pleasures of philosophy.

10. He is happier when he is a private citizen.

Suggested Essay Topics

1. Defend one of the four "degenerate" characters as having the most pleasant life. Include and respond to Plato's critique of this life.

2. Is philosophy the highest good? Why does Plato think it is? Construct an alternate highest good and defend it against philosophy.

Book Ten

1. Critique of Art (595–605b)

Summary

Socrates reemphasizes the importance of the limits placed on poetry in the city in speech. Artists' products are only imitations of reality, twice removed from the true characteristic of the world of forms. Artists' (specifically poets') claims to have broad knowledge about mankind are false. Socrates supports his claim by showing that nothing of value has come from Homer's writings and that poets have not been men of action. Poets cannot be true educators because they do not know what is good.

Since artists neither use nor create the objects they depict, their representations lack the benefit of expert knowledge. For this reason, concludes Socrates, artists have no true standards to guide what they produce. This leads them to choose as their standard public opinion, a critique that above all applies to the tragic poets. Furthermore, because representing the actions of the reasoning element of the brain is difficult, as well as boring to the public, dramatic poets focus on representing the lower elements. This encourages these bad elements in the individual as well as the state. It is therefore right to exclude poetry from the good state.

Analysis

According to Desmond Lee, this section has been inserted into the *Republic* in order to strengthen its earlier critique of poetry "against anticipated or actual criticism" (Lee, 1974:421). This time

Plato's argument is strengthened by its reference to the theory of forms, as expressed in the simile of the divided line. Plato's description of artistic works as representations of physical objects places them, and their creators, furthest from the perfect world of forms. Since they look neither to knowledge (of the forms) or to expertise (valid in the material world), artists and their creations can only be full of ignorance (the characteristic mentality of the lowest end of the divided line).

Plato's parting shot is to compare the artists to Sophists. Using language similar to the metaphor of the animal trainer, Plato says artists can't tell good from bad and use popularity as their only standard of merit. Modern critics have instead found Greek dramatists to have produced profound critiques of the polis. Plato's critique might as well be aimed at the variety of dramatists' visions, which would be very subversive in the context of the enforced unity of the city in speech.

2. Exclusion of Poetry from the Ideal City (605c–608b)

Summary

Poetry has a tremendous power to corrupt because it can make a man enjoy behavior that he would normally be ashamed of. By allowing oneself to be moved by drama, one weakens one's own control over the low and unseemly emotions, such as sadness, gaiety, lust, and anger. For this reason, one should pity those who call Homer the educator of Greece, remembering that if the state does not exclude most poetry, "pleasure and pain will jointly be kings in your city instead of law" (607a). The only poetry that should be allowed is hymns to the gods and songs in praise of good men. One must constantly remind oneself that most poetry is far from Truth and guard that it not insinuate itself into one's soul.

Analysis

Plato's discussion of Homer in this section reinforces the modern readers' sense of the role he had in Greek society. In the previous section, Plato discounted the technical knowledge for which

Homer received credit. Now he focuses on the misguided moral lessons the *Iliad* contains, addressing himself to the just man instead of the needs of the just city. His message is that the well-harmonized man must reject the many bad lessons taught by Homer and other writers, instead keeping his focus on self-control and, of course, philosophy.

3. The Immortality of the Soul (608c–612a)

Summary

Socrates begins a description of the rewards of being good. He first asserts that the soul is immortal. Everything has a peculiar evil that causes it to degenerate. The soul must therefore be immortal because none of the evils that beset it can destroy it. Vice only degrades the soul.

Plato then adds that the soul is shown to be beautiful by its love of wisdom, but that the earthly pursuits most men choose to engage in obscure its essential purity.

Analysis

Plato's simile comparing the soul to the sea-god Glaucus is another example of Plato's tremendous poetic skills. Glaucus, according to Bloom, was a fisherman who became a god after he threw himself into the sea. Plato describes the condition of the soul encrusted with the baggage of mortal cares as similar to the monstrosity Glaucus became after enough sea life attached itself to what was once a human form.

4. The Benefits of Justice: The Myth of Er (612b–621)

Summary

Socrates concludes that justice is its own reward. He then begins a discussion of the worldly and divine benefits that accompany justice.

According to Socrates, the gods love only the just man. If a just man suffers, it is all a plan for his future benefit. The unjust man

may flourish initially, but the just man will end up with reputation and wealth in the long run. Justice triumphs and injustice is punished on earth.

A just man can anticipate even greater rewards after his death. To illustrate, Socrates tells the story of Er, a warrior who came back to life 12 days after his death, just before his funeral pyre was to be lit. Er said he had been sent back by the gods to tell mankind what awaited them after they died. In the realm of the dead, Er saw judges split the new arrivals into the just and the unjust. Er heard that those who had committed evil deeds were punished tenfold for their evils, while the good were rewarded tenfold for their kind deeds. The very worst souls were flayed and carded upon a field of thorns before being thrown into the Tartarus.

Socrates then describes Er's vision of the structure of the universe, which consisted of interlocking spheres revolving around the axis of Necessity. Er saw the three fates within these spheres, giving out lots to the arriving spirits, which determined the order in which they would choose their next lives. There was a great variety of lives, both human and animal, from which they could choose according to their own desires. Socrates here notes the importance of having pursued philosophy in one's life, for without the special knowledge it gives, one will never be able to properly choose a good life at this stage. This problem is especially pronounced in those who have been good through habit and not philosophy.

Er watched an assortment of famous characters, such as Orpheus and Agammemnon, choose their new lives in reaction to the events of their past lives. He then accompanied the souls through the plain of Lethe (forgetfulness), where they were given a drink from the river of Carelessness, which washed their knowledge away. At midnight, each soul was sent off to be born anew, except for Er, who was sent back to his body to tell this tale for mankind's edification.

Socrates says the lesson of this story is that we should always pursue lives of justice. This will keep us at peace internally and with the gods, rewarding us in the afterlife as well as on the long journey on the earth.

Analysis

Plato neatly ties up his book with references to Cephalus, the elderly man who briefly discussed justice in the beginning of the *Republic*. Cephalus has led an essentially just life, for which he has been rewarded with peace of mind in his old age. Yet Plato finds his just actions wanting because they do not have a philosophical basis. Without it, Plato says, one may choose one's next life poorly. Thus, even the man who is already good should study philosophy.

It is most ironic that after his defense of the value of justice, Plato should tack on these passages about the benefits of justice, as if he were more concerned with getting people actually to practice it than to get them to understand it. Beyond its material benefits, praised in 612–613, Plato extols justice's benefits in the afterlife and the tenfold punishment that will follow injustice. Thus, the final lesson of the *Republic* is not that justice should be practiced because it is good for the soul, but that it should be practiced for its concrete benefits in the material world and the inevitability of punishment for bad actions.

While Plato has spent much time criticizing the poets, there is no doubt that he has created a strong poetry in the many myths of the *Republic*. But his stories contrast with those he has criticized because of their intentional lessons. While Homer created a beautiful work of art out of the myths and history he wove with poetry to become the *Iliad*, he might have made different choices if he knew his story were to become the foundation stone of Hellas.

Plato's myths are liberated from mythology and history; they arise indigenously with the sole purpose of teaching the higher truths that lead to the improvement of the state and of the individual. The Golden Lie provides an artificial familial unity that would have gone far to eliminating strife in Sparta. Cloaked as a myth, it would have been a powerful force against the abuse and corruption that ate away Spartan society. The Allegory of the Cave, while meant to illuminate Plato's system of forms, has an educative value that transcends one man's philosophy; the modern citizen finds it a reminder to question one's assumptions continually about the nature of things. Finally, the Myth of Er cements in the reader's mind the necessity of leading a just life (and a philosophical life if one is capable). This lesson serves the Athenian state, the ideal state, and the modern state well, for justice provides peace, an element of statecraft that has timeless value.

Plato's myths are beautifully written and remarkably instructive. With them he challenges the poets on their own territory and succeeds by artistically making the case for the value of a just life in the state, the soul, the present, and the future. It is for this artistry as much for Plato's philosophy that the *Republic* stands as a classic of Western civilization.

Study Questions

1. To what two things do the number of spheres correspond?

2. Why might a just man suffer?

3. Why is the creation of an artisan closer to truth than the creation of an artist?

4. How does poetry weaken the mind?

5. Why does the first soul to choose its next incarnation in the Myth of Er make a bad decision?

6. In what way are the goals of the dramatist and the rhetor–itician similar?

7. Who are Lachesis, Clotho, and Atropos?

8. Why is Odysseus' choice wise?

9. In what two things does Socrates find proof of the soul's immortality?

10. To which section of the line do artists' works correspond?

Answers

1. The number of spheres corresponds, first, to the heavenly bodies visible to the Greeks and, second, to the notes of a scale.

2. A just man might suffer for the sins of his past life. His suffering will always be with an eye on his future benefit, in this life or the next.

3. An artisan looks to expert opinion when making his objects, while the artist only looks to public opinion.

4. Poetry weakens the mind because it deliberately appeals to the lower elements, and people choose to let themselves be swayed by its appeal.

5. He had previously been good through habit and not through philosophy, so he chose the life of a tyrant—only to discover that he would wind up eating his children.

6. They both aim to please the public.

7. They are the three Fates.

8. Odysseus' choice is wise because he was cured of ambition and chose a life that, while dull, would give him happiness.

9. Socrates finds proof of the soul's immortality in the absence of an agent that can destroy it and in the soul's love of wisdom.

10. Artists' works correspond to the lowest section of the line, the one that corresponds to the mental condition of ignorance.

Suggested Essay Topics

1. Examining the *Republic* as a whole, explain whether Plato's view of human nature is that it is essentially good or essentially evil.

2. Explain Socrates' argument in favor of justice for its own sake. Is this strong enough to defeat the definitions of justice presented at the beginning of the *Republic*?

SECTION TWELVE

Sample Analytical Paper Topics

The following paper topics are designed to test your understanding of the *Republic* as a whole and your ability to analyze important themes, concepts, and devices. Following each question is a sample outline to help get you started.

Topic #1

Many modern democratic theorists consider Athens in its Golden Age to be a model of democratic practice. Plato, however, is highly critical of his society's form of government. How does the *Republic* criticize Athenian democracy? Is Plato's critique valid?

Outline

I. Thesis Statement: *Despite the modern praise of Athens for being a more democratic society than any today, Plato is highly critical of his government. Plato is right / wrong to criticize the democratic practice of ancient Athens.*

II. Description of Athenian Democracy

    A. All male citizens are eligible to participate.

    B. Any citizen can speak in the Assembly.

    C. Offices are filled by lot.

III. Plato's Critique

    A. Democracy panders to low desires.

        1. Description of the three elements of the soul

    2. Parallel to Athenian society

    3. Metaphor of the animal trainer

  B. Democracy fosters rule by the ignorant.

    1. Hierarchy of knowledge is established in the simile of the line.

    2. Allegory of the Cave

  C. Exclusion of the best rulers

    1. Society views the "star gazer" as useless.

    2. Society corrupts the young philosopher.

IV. Plato is right / wrong because:

  A. Knowledge is / is not required for good rule.

  B. Democracy does / does not pander to low desires.

  C. Philosophers would / would not be the best rulers.

Topic #2

Plato's, and more specifically the *Republic's*, role in literature has most often been as a source of allegories. Examine three of Plato's allegories as recounted by Socrates in the *Republic*. What lesson is each supposed to teach?

Outline

I. Thesis Statement: *Plato's memorable allegories serve to enable the reader to more clearly understand his philosophy.*

II. Ship of State

  A. Description of the captain, crew, and navigator

  B. Parallel to Athenian society

  C. Lesson: Only the "star gazer" (the philosopher) can properly lead the state. It is foolish to ignore him and assume oneself to be wiser than he.

III. The Animal Trainer

    A. Description of the animal and its trainer

    B. Parallel to Athenian society

    C. Shortcomings: The trainer never encourages the animal to do what is right, only to follow its tastes.

    D. Lesson: Those who lead society must transcend their assumptions about human nature or risk failing as leaders: the leaders should do what is right, not what is popular.

IV. The Cave

    A. Description of the Cave, the prisoners, and the escapee

    B. Parallel to Athenian society

    C. Lesson: Only the philosopher has the knowledge. While he may try to enlighten others as to their condition, his knowledge will often be discounted by those whose lives are based on illusion.

Topic #3

The original theme of the *Republic* is the nature of justice. Describe three conceptions of justice presented in the text, elaborating on Socrate's parallels between justice in the individual and justice in society. Which concept is best, and why? Where does each fail?

Outline

I. Thesis Statement: *Of the many concepts of justice presented in the* Republic, *the most sound is that of* _____.

II. Justice According to Polemarchus

    A. Justice is giving to each what is due to him or her.

    B. Justice allows harming one's enemies and helping one's friends.

    C. Failing: Such a narrow definition may lead to unjust actions.

D. Failing: This concept is not entirely based upon doing what is right.

III. Justice According to Thrasymachus

A. Might makes right: It is right that the weak should be dominated by the strong.

B. The person best at dominating others is happiest.

C. Failing: There is no guarantee that the actions of the tyrant will be in his or her best interest.

D. Failing: The personality theory involved may not be true.

E. Failing: No alternate understanding of "happiness" is allowed.

IV. The Best Definition of Justice

A. The best definition of justice is that presented by _____.

B. Its failings are outweighed by its advantages. For example, while it is a shortcoming that _____'s theory might lead to _____, it is more important that it would lead to _____.

C. _____'s theory is also better than the other two because _____.

Bibliography

Finely, M. I. *The Ancient Greeks*. (1963) 1987. New York: Peregrine Books.

Kitto, H. D. F. *The Greeks*. (1951) 1991. New York: Penguin Books.

Plato. *The Republic*. Translation and commentary by Desmond Lee. (1955) 1974. New York: Penguin Books.

Plato. *The Republic*. Translation and commentary by Allan Bloom. (1968) 1991. New York: Basic Books.

Warner, Rex. *The Greek Philosophers*. 1958. New York: Mentor.

A Glance at Some of the Characters

Plato

Socrates

Glaucon

Thrasymachus

Male Guardian

Female Guardian

Three Social Classes

Homer